Dan's Trees

Written by Jenny Feely

Illustrated by Chantal Stewart

Flying Start
to Literacy®

Contents

Chapter 1
First day of school

The first day at a new school was hard. Jake knew all about that. He'd had nine first days at different schools already. Jake's dad worked for a timber company. His job was to help cut down forests so the timber could be used to make things. When all the usable trees in one area had been cut down, Jake's dad had to move on, and Jake had to move with him.

This move had been better than most. They had moved back to the area where Dad had grown up, so they were living with Jake's grandpa. It was good for Jake to have some more family around – especially since Mum had died.

But the first day at school would still be hard. Jake got on the school bus, walked to the back and sat down. Everyone stared at him. No one smiled. No one spoke. Just like all the other first days.

Jake tried not to look at all the other kids on the bus. He got out his camera and started looking through his latest shots. Taking photos was something Jake was good at. He always had his camera with him.

Just as the bus was about to take off, a boy came racing toward it.

"Wait for me!" yelled the boy, leaping onto the bus and heading for the back seat.

"I nearly missed it – again!" he said, sitting next to Jake. He glanced at the camera. "Wow, those photos are good."

And just like that, Jake and Dan were friends.

"I'm always late," Dan said. "Today I was making a sign for my tree house and I forgot about the time."

"A tree house?" said Jake. "Cool!"

"Yeah, it's okay," said Dan. "But the tree it's in is pretty special."

"Why?" said Jake. "Trees are all the same."

"You won't say that when you see it," said Dan.

Chapter 2
The promise

After school that day, Jake and Dan set off to see the tree house.

At first they walked through the clear cut area that Jake's dad had been working in. With all the trees cut down it looked bare and gloomy. Then they walked along the track to Ferny Creek. But when they reached a big rock that looked like a bear, Dan stopped.

"Before I show you my tree house, you have to promise you won't tell anyone where it is," he said.

"Okay," said Jake. "I promise."

Dan pushed back a fallen branch to reveal a narrow, winding path.

"Follow me," said Dan, as he took off down the hidden track.

The path took them deeper and deeper into the forest. Then suddenly Dan stepped out into a sunny clearing.

In the middle of the clearing was the biggest tree that Jake had ever seen.

"How do you like my
tree house?" said Dan,
pointing at the giant tree.

"Wow!" said Jake.
"It's amazing."

And it was. The tree seemed to touch the sky and it had an enormous trunk. There were massive trees all around the clearing. Jake began taking photos.

"Stop!" said Dan. "You can't take photos! No one knows these trees are here. If the timber company saw those photos, they'd come looking for the trees."

"They don't know about them?" asked Jake.

"No," said Dan. "This place is hard to get to and that cliff hides the trees from the helicopters searching for new areas to log."

"Don't worry," said Jake, "I won't show these photos to anyone. They're just for us."

From then on Jake and Dan went to the tree house almost every day. It was their favourite place in the world. Until one day Jake got some news he had been dreading.

Chapter 3
Bad news

Jake came home to find Dad and Grandpa in the workshop. Dad was home early, and that always meant the same thing. They were moving – again.

"Noooo!" groaned Jake. "Not again."

"I'm sorry," said Dad. "But I have to go where the big trees are, and all the big trees around here have been cut down. It's time for us to leave."

"I don't want to go," said Jake, tears pricking the backs of his eyes.

"I don't either," said Dad. "But my job is with the forests and trees."

"Come here, Jake," said Grandpa. "I want to show you something."

Jake hesitated, then went to sit with Grandpa.

"We're making this table top from one enormous piece of wood," said Grandpa. "It came from a massive old tree, wider than this room."

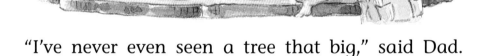

"I've never even seen a tree that big," said Dad.

"Neither have I," said Grandpa. "But my grandpa did – right here in the valley. It was full of those trees before the logging began."

"Really?" asked Dad. "Trees like that are very rare, and worth a lot of money to timber companies."

And that was when Jake had an idea. An idea that was wonderful and terrible at the same time.

All night Jake tossed and turned. What should he do? He didn't want to move away. Living with Grandpa was great. But he didn't want to break his promise either – Dan was the best friend he'd ever had. But if they moved away, how would he and Dan stay friends? Jake went over it in his head again and again.

But in the morning when he saw the school
bus coming down the road, Jake made up
his mind. He turned around and headed home.
He didn't see Dan on the bus, waving at him,
as the bus slowed down.

Dad and Grandpa looked up in surprise as
Jake walked in the door.

"I've got something to show you," said Jake.
"Something that will mean we don't have
to move."

Jake led Grandpa and Dad through the
forest and behind the bear-shaped rock.

"Are you sure you know where you're going?"
asked Dad.

"Yep!" said Jake. But that was the only
thing he was sure about.

They followed the track deep down into the valley, finally stepping into the clearing with the massive old trees.

"Will you look at that," said Grandpa.

"They are amazing," said Dad. "These trees would be worth a lot of money to the timber company."

And that was when Dan stepped out from inside the tree house.

"Liar!" Dan screamed at Jake. "I trusted you."

"What! How did you know I would be here?" asked Jake, his face turning pale.

"I saw you from the bus. But when you turned around, I wanted to find out if you were okay. So I got off the bus and went to your house. When no one was there, I thought you might be here."

"I'm so sorry," said Jake. "I didn't know
what else to do. I don't want to move away.
You're the best friend I've ever had."

"You're not my friend. Friends don't lie,"
yelled Dan, running out of the clearing.

"What have I done?" said Jake, sinking to
the ground and watching his friend run off.

Grandpa turned to Dad. "It would be a shame to cut down such wonderful old giants," he said. "The timber from these trees might be worth a lot of money, but surely a living forest must be worth something too!"

Jake couldn't even look at his father. One word from Dad and the timber company would come and cut down the trees.

Dad looked thoughtfully from Grandpa to Jake, then he walked slowly around the big old trees.

"I didn't believe such trees still existed," said Dad quietly. "Now that I see how special they are, I have to protect them. I have to stop them from being cut down – even if it costs me my job."

Jake looked up at Dad hopefully.

"The timber company doesn't know these trees are here," said Dad. "Let's keep it that way."

Chapter 4
Saying sorry

Jake was silent all the way home. Dan's trees were safe, but now they would have to move away – away from Grandpa and away from Dan. There would be another town and another first day at school.

Jake figured he deserved it after what he had done. But before they left, he had to let Dan know that the trees were safe.

He tried calling but Dan wouldn't take his calls. He went to Dan's house but Dan refused to come to the door.

Jake didn't know what to do. He sat on his bed and did what he always did when he was feeling sad – he flicked through his photos. And there it was – the picture of Dan in front of his tree house. This gave Jake an idea. He printed the picture and wrote on the back.

Dan
I did the wrong thing and I am very sorry. But I want you to know that the trees are safe. Dad is not going to fell the timber.

Jake knew that if he left the photo for Dan and someone else saw it then the secret would be out anyway – and it would still be Jake's fault. He walked into the kitchen.

"Have we got an envelope big enough for this?" he asked, showing Grandpa the photo.

"Where did you get that?" Grandpa asked.

"I took it with my camera," said Jake.

"Well, it's a mighty fine photo," said Grandpa. "And it gives me an idea."

Jake wanted to know what the idea was, but Grandpa wouldn't say. Grandpa went to find Dad, and the two of them sat and talked long into the night.

"We need your photo of Dan's tree house," said Dad the next morning.

"Why?" asked Jake suspiciously.

"We want to keep Dan's trees safe forever," said Grandpa. "And we figure that the best way to do that is to show people how amazing they are. If enough people want them protected, they'll be safe."

"And Jake," said Dad. "We're not moving. Grandpa and I are going to work together. We are going to start a new business and we are going to try to save those trees."

Jake was happy that he and Dad were going to stay in the valley and live with Grandpa. But he knew it would never be the same without Dan as his friend. Maybe, he thought, one day Dan might be my friend again. But he knew it would be a long time before that happened.

Postscript

Dan's trees were saved.

Jake's grandfather took samples of the trees and, along with Jake's photos, sent them to the National Society for the Protection of Trees. There was only one other forest known to have this species of tree.

The society sent scientists to take further samples to confirm the species. These trees are now listed as an endangered species.

Jake's dad no longer works for the timber company. He and his father set up a tourism company that takes groups into the valley to see the giant old trees. People come from all over the country and sometimes from other countries to see the trees.

And Dan did forgive Jake, and they have been friends ever since.

A note from the author

I once saw a picture of a hollow tree stump that was so big it had been used as a stable for 12 horses. I began to wonder... what if there was one last group of giant old trees left in that area? Who would know about it? What would happen if the forestry industry knew the trees were there? And so my story began to take shape.

I also started to think about some children I know who have had to change schools many times because of the work their parents do, and how hard it can be for these children to make friends.

When I put these two ideas together, I had my story.